Random Saints

Random Saints

Poems by

Joe Cottonwood

Cover design by Shay Culligan
Cover art by Sarah White

ISBN: 978-1-952326-21-9

Kelsay Books
502 South 1040 East, A-119
American Fork, Utah, 84003

Acknowledgments

With the exception of the section "Salvage," all of these poems have appeared in journals. My deep thanks go to the following editors for giving these poems their first publication.

Leslee Goodman of *MOON*

Firestone Feinberg of *Verse-Virtual*

Carmel Mawle of *Dove Tales*

Sally Long of *Allegro*

Cristina Norcross of *Blue Heron Review*

Wren Tuatha of *Califragile*

Jeannie E. Roberts of *Halfway Down the Stairs*

Vern Miller of *Fifth Wednesday*

Zvi A. Sesling of *Muddy River Poetry Review*

Russell Streur of *Plum Tree Tavern*

Katherine Smith of *Potomac Review*

Roderick Bates of *Rat's Ass Review*

Corey Cook of *Red Eft Review*

Shannon Connor Winward of *Riddled With Arrows*

Sonia Greenfield of *Rise Up Review*

Judith Lawrence of *River Poets Journal*

Leila Rae of *riverbabble*

Mary Crockett Hill of *Roanoke Review*

Jeffrey & Tobi Alfier of *San Pedro River Review*

Dan Sicoli of *Slipstream*

Jacinta V. White of *Snapdragon*

Diana Christine of *Spirit First*

Pratibha Kelapure of *The Literary Nest*

David Jibson of *Third Wednesday*

Nancy Scott of *US 1 Worksheets*

Bill Siverly of *Windfall*

David LaBounty of *Workers Write!*

Jayne Jaudon Ferrer of *Your Daily Poem*

and the editors of *Indian River Review*

Contents

Call of Nature

The Opposite of Hate

Random Saints

English as a Second Language

Twenty adults, all Vietnamese,
sit respectfully in a classroom,
San Jose City College, silent.
The point is to talk (in English).
The instructor asks, "How did you get here?"
Hesitantly, first one:
      She walked a hundred kilometers
      carrying two children, paid a boatman,
      too many people, boat sank, a child drowned.
Next one:
      Attacked by pirates, daughter stolen,
      never seen again.
Then an outpouring:
      Typhus. An ambush. Cheated.
      An angel in the form of a helicopter.
Courage, heartbreak, luck.
And plenty of talk.

Next class.
"What is the most beautiful
sight you've ever beheld?"
They traveled, reluctantly, half the planet.
What splendors passed their eyes?
A hesitation, then the first:
      "Most beautiful I ever see
      is San Jose Airport."
Immediately a chorus, they all agree.
First glimpse, descending from broken clouds.
      Tarmac. Landing lights.
      San Jose Airport.
      Beauty.

The Diplomat's Daughter

She can recite the 23rd Psalm in Hindi,
once drank Coca Cola with Martin Luther King,
is 11 years old. I'm 14. The year is 1961.
Public school, we're the same grade.
I'm not brilliant, she says. *I'm experienced.*
We ride the bus. She sits with me,
walks with me after I rescue her once from
certain ignorant assholes. In a white school
she's skinny and shy and brown.

Her father sizes me up, says *You can be her big brother.*
I get the drift: *Don't you dare touch her.* No worries.
She knows embassy protocols—when to shake hands,
when to curtsy, when to kiss both cheeks. I know
the secret map of where to sit safely in the cafeteria.
She says *We can't save the world. But we can serve it.*

Somewhere between September and April
she grows less skinny, more female. One day
she takes my hand when we're walking
and says *In June we're moving to Singapore.*
Sudden pain like stomach gas. I guess it shows.
I am not your little sister, she says. *Do you love me?*
At that age I'm compulsively honest,
so I say *I don't know what love is.*
THIS, she says. *What you feel right now is love.*

We hold hands, kiss a few times,
sweet stuff, both of us shy, she for once
as inexperienced as I. Last day she presses
my hand to her heart, her little breast and says
I'll miss you. I'm scared. Goodbye.

A postcard, exotic stamp. Just kids,
we lose touch. So 40 years pass
until her photo, name in the news:
car-bombed fighting polio in Pakistan.
Served the world. Couldn't save it.
In human culture there's no secret map
of where to sit, where to not.
Only *THIS,* what we must feel.

Hospital, Indiana

Phil is so restless, Air Force vet,
big black beard, hates hippies
though he looks like one.
"Flag-burners," he calls them.
From war he learned: "Life changes fast."

As tech support Phil has seen every corner
of this hospital, pulled every wire.
Hear that scream? Burn patient, little girl
in physical therapy, breaks Phil's heart.
Want a poker game? Always one in the morgue.
Walk into the autopsy room, you might see
a doc pulling parts from a man's chest
like lifting the head gasket on a Jeep.
"Death never changes," Phil says.
"And it sucks."

In the recovery room where people go after surgery
this hippie nurse is changing an IV bottle over one man
when another goes into convulsions
so the nurse drops the bottle on the first man's chest
and he grunts and passes out while she runs
to the spasm guy. There's no other staff.
Phil says, "Um, I'll come back later
to fix your terminal," but the nurse with big dark eyes
makes a pleading face, so Phil holds the bottle.

That night he sees her waiting for a bus
clutching herself like a freezing gypsy in tears
because the guy with convulsions just died
so he gives her a ride home but first
he takes her bowling, she needs it. Life changes fast.
Turns out they both love bowling,
who'da thunk it?

A peacenik and a flyboy.
Hospitals heal people, sometimes.
"Now we got three kids. We all go bowling.
Good karma, ya know?"

The Family Tree

From this tree, they lynched John T
for the crime of preaching against slavery.
Hollow now, like a scolding ghost
this spar stands among Holsteins
in the pasture of a man who figures
we're cousins somehow.
He, a midwestern farmer,
me, a California craftsman,
political poles apart but
blood is thicker than geography.

Tough to salvage, ancient black walnut
riddled by woodpecker, softened by rot.
Working together with chain saw and wrecking bar
we find a section of solid core.
Here's a scar in the bark like a grinning face
where the branch broke off, long gone.
That happy limb held the rope
swinging John T's massive frame
of muscle and blubber and bluster.
Until it snapped. And he ran.
Fast as a fat man could run.

John T, grandfather of my grandfather,
ran into the forest hiding until his best friend
rescued him, a man named, ironically, Lynch,
grandfather of the grandfather of the man
with whom I speak. Thus,
cousins in the country way.

I'll make salad bowls, I say,
wooden forks and tongs, walnut plates,
maybe even a tea set for your daughter
who seems so outspoken, so feisty and strong.
Tea set? he says, she needs a lectern!

So here it is.
The grinning knot on the surface.
Those holes in the side, from bullets.
Lead slugs. I dug them out.
Here, this cloth sack.
May she heft them in her fist.
May her words fire like cannons
for freedom.

A Random Saint Rides the Bus

With a face of wretched scars like layered pond scum
in the seat beside me she says without prompting
    "I teach seventh grade social studies
    because I love to bend a mind like molten metal
    before it cools hard. Hm. Hm-mum."

She hums one, two notes like commas
as she talks, tuning her thoughts.
    "My cubs, that age, the hormones hit so hard
    you can hear their heartbeats.
    Beat-beat, so loud. Hm.
    Hm hm. My cubs, every day
    they navigate among the flotsam.
    Just look at this bus. What they deal with.
    And you and me, right? Because
    we're all riding on this bus. Hm-mum.

    "My cubs don't know their values.
    They may not know their own gender.
    It's a race to develop personal integrity
    before the peer group kills them. Hm.
    They need somebody who will listen
    to their heartbeats. Somebody must say
    'Yes that's right'
    or 'No that's absolutely wrong'
    though mostly I say 'There's no absolute here'
    but I love those emerging souls and maybe
    I help shape them in some small way. Hm. Hm.

"You wonder what happened to my face?
One of my cubs threw acid.
One of my lost ones.
Hm hm hm."
A thin gold chain around her neck,
a gold cross upon her chest.
"Here's my stop" she says.
"Have a great day."

sand

flowers tingle my fingers
leaves crunch a bunch crinkly
a giant camper van in a driveway
door locked
pebbles and bricks never get sick
caw caw crows
sand between toes
where does sand come from?

pumpkins on front steps faces like mean people
big black fuzzy spider on a fence
I'm not scared they eat bad bugs
carpenters banging on a house

here's the library which has
headphones to put over ears
color books to pull off shelves
checkout machine needs a card
yes I'll go now

listen it's a leaf blower not a lawnmower
in this garden a little tower of bells
you can ring with your fingers ting ting
a yard full of rocks some broken some whole
this stone is perfect so smooth I'll keep in my pocket
just a stone not stealing only just one
the giant camper van in a driveway
door locked

once I had a driveway
sunset so many colors
smell of rain
pardon my cough
where does sand come from?

Homeless Encampment

Excuse me, sir,
but did you once
come upon three Cub Scouts
in blue uniforms wandering lost in a small forest
hearing bears in the underbrush, vultures in the sky
and you guided us to daylight
where no one had missed us?
Oh. Well, anyway,
let me give you a beer.

Pardon me, ma'am,
but did you once
substitute-teach a high school English class
the subject was poetry but you only knew limericks
and the class was in stitches;
you made us promise not to tell
but they never hired you again?
Oh. Well, anyway,
let me give you a beer.

So sorry, sir,
but did you once
as a night watchman come upon
a boy and a girl kissing without clothing
in the factory shadow in your flashlight beam
and you said "Don't make a mess"
and moved on?
Oh. Well, anyway,
let me give you a beer. Three beers
and I'll show you pictures of some
fine little messes, grown big and gone away.

Vietnam Memorial, Washington, DC

Simple folk
(and here we are all simple folk)
set tokens at a wall lined with names.
Flowers, framed photos, a note:
> *Happy Birthday*
> *Angel GrandDaddy*
> *from Teresa.*
Everyone combs the names. It's what one does here.

I find Denny.
Oh man. That was fifty years ago.
This life, he hasn't had.
Can't find Jimmy. Guess he made it, after all.
Wet eyes. I have to sit down.

You, little one, without a word
climb onto my lap, lean your cheek
against my chest, breathing. My love.
Just right.
After so much went wrong.

Salvage

Here's to the Fragrance of Concrete

Here's to the fragrance of concrete
  as it cures.

Yes I said fragrance—
  damp
    yet oddly dusty,
  petrichor of first raindrops.

As you can smell an oncoming storm
  here is the aroma
    of pending permanence,
  a spirit peaceful, unloved.

Honor the skilled arms,
  the corded legs and hairy backs,
    the labor that shaped
  this puddle of stone.

Inhale, savor the dignity of concrete—
  the humility, the brawn,
    the gray bouquet.

Ode to a Leather Tool Belt

I've junked three trucks and still I keep you.
Buried five dogs. Raised three children.
And still I wear you.

You jingle when I walk. Nails clink in pouches.
The drill in its holster slaps my leg.
The hammer in its clip spanks my butt.
You bristle with screwdrivers, chisel,
big fat pencil, needle-nose plier.
You call attention. Random kids follow asking
"What are you doing?" Then: "Can I help?"

You smell like me (and I, like you).
Leather, fourth decade.
I've washed your pouches with saddle soap,
sewn your seams with dental floss.
Now the web of your belt is fraying,
wrapped with duct tape.

Your pockets fill over time. Once in a while
I remove every tool, every last screw and nail.
I hold you upside down and shake.
Sawdust, a dead spider, little strippings
of insulated wire will fall out.
And once, my missing wedding ring.
I had taken it to a jeweler for repair,
but when I got there couldn't find it.
A year later, you coughed it up.

When your webbing finally snaps,
when you drop from my waist,
maybe it's you, old tool belt, I'll take
to the jeweler for remounting,
for buff and polish. He'll understand.

Because

Because that day, son,
for a family's Apple II (a computer, son, in 1981),
to run wires in their crawlspace I had to
wiggle-waggle over rat shit,
wibble-wobble over broken glass,
writhe through cobwebs
and squirm into a concrete hole,

Because
I also de-jammed their garbage disposal,

Because
they had a nearly naked teenage daughter (July, hot day)
with a deep suntan and braces in her teeth
who apologized for dropping all those rubber bands
into the disposal and who then kept hovering,
asking questions, licking lips, leaning forward,
testing her budding sexuality when she knew all I
would do, *could* do was answer her remarks and
gaze once or twice into those starry brown eyes,

Because that same day
the family next door asked me to make an estimate
on building a darkroom in their baking-hot garage
where two teenage boys were hanging out making
crude remarks about the budding parts of girl-next-door,
more goddamn pubescent sexuality,

Because
I asked if they even knew her eye color
and they said no; if they knew she had a pet hamster
and again they said no; if they'd ever talked to her
and they said no;

      Because
I told them you should learn her eyes
as an astronomer learns the galaxies;
you should befriend her hamster named Gummy
who is the moon in her orbit;
and don't you dare touch that girl's Milky Way
until she's older and don't you *ever* dare hurt her;
and they regarded me like some weird wrathful god
but I bet they'll respect her (and make snickering jokes
about me when I'm gone, the grease of my shirt,
the black in my fingerprints, the motes of fiberglass
insulation in my hair),

      Because that evening
I come home stinking and itching,
too late for dinner from a long hot hectic day
with $80 earned,

      And then because, son, that night
after tucking the kids who are now
your two older sisters into bed,

      After a silent prayer
for your other sister who was born and died
all in one day,

      After I strip off my clothes
and take a long steaming soak
in our claw-footed bathtub,

After toweling dry
I find your mother penciling a crossword puzzle in bed,
and she says she's fertile,
and I had just cooked every tiny tadpole in my sac,

    though it seems
one of those tiny tadpoles,
a clean and well-soaked one
still retained a wee bit of wiggle,
a Y chromosome wiggle wobble writhe.

    You were a glorious teenager.
A stargazer. You, a man now,
with a lifelong love
of hot tubs and hot springs.
    Because.

Like Pigs

It's Janice on the phone
from her sailboat near Madagascar
(sound of waves slapping hull
half a planet distant). Her tenants
have a stopped-up sink,
their own fault says Janice because
they live like pigs packing five kids
into that two-bedroom cottage
but I should fix it which is how
I meet freckly smiley Georgia
who is discretely nursing a blanketed babe
as she leads me to the one and only bathroom
where opening the sink cabinet I find
giant brown fungi in a pool of slime.

Georgia says *Yikes!*
Baby starts fussing
probably about the smell
like raccoon turd pudding.
I have to scrape out fungus,
run a snake through black goo,
then straighten the drain
which was never installed properly
causing the whole problem.

Georgia is stirring soup over a stove,
babe in arms like a copper cherub
while four kids of laddering ages
play kick the can. Tom arrives
in his old truck, joins the game.
Georgia calls to him
You done it for today?
Tom shouts back
I replaced a windshield wiper
on Bradley's car, he don't know.
Georgia explains to me Tom's a mechanic,
performs a secret good deed each day.
It's so simple, she says.

Back to the bathroom, quickly
I replace the crappy shower nozzle.
I won't ask.
Janice won't pay.
Like pigs we nurture, we bless.

She (a girl!) was the best finish carpenter

we'd ever seen. Her age, seventeen.
Learned the trade from her dad.
After hazing (nothing nasty),
we sort of normalized her. Sort of not.
Found reasons to be within sight of her for crown
molding as she was short and had to stretch—until
she called us creepy and we stopped. But, jeez,
hanging a door was like a ballet, strength and grace.
Not classic beauty, more stocky and square.
We gave her the tasks where perfect would count.
Because she was.

By end of summer we all treated her
like a kid sister. She brought Vivaldi
for the boom box to replace our twangy slop.
She chalked little flowers, hearts and dragonflies
in the rough opening before trimming the frame
so in demolition a century from now
somebody might find them.
Earned enough for first semester at college.
Promised she'd come back and visit.

Maybe she forgot.
Maybe she met some brooding poet.
We speak of her sometimes after all these years.
It's like opening a wall,
finding a chalk dragonfly.

Salvage: Gilda

Gilda makes documentary films,
you may have seen them.
She hires me as on-call handyman
to expunge scissors stuck in toilet drains,
plastic ponies melted in wall heaters,
a campfire built on a hardwood floor.
As I work (for years) she brings me coffee;
as I depart she says
Without you I would sell this madhouse.

I'm replacing a garbage disposal
in the kitchen when I see out the window
the daughter drama queen
(now grown to age thirteen)
with a boy, a hairy-chested older boy.
They disrobe—all the way. I set down my wrench.
They climb into the hot tub where they begin
to cuddle and—oh my. I step into the yard.
The boy leaps from the tub and sprints trampling
the garden. Over a fence, privates flapping.
In a puddle at my feet sit his clothes.
In the air, scent of chlorine and patchouli.
Look away, the daughter says, and I do.
Rustling shirt and jeans over wetness she says
If you tell my mom, I'll say it was you.
I'll say you tried to rape me.

But I tell.
Gilda rolls her eyes.
Not again, Gilda says.

From the back of my truck I'm searching
for a box of drywall screws when I see
Gilda's athlete-nerd son running
pell-mell down the sidewalk.
Lord, he's fast.
But the boy pursuing
is faster and catches him by the collar,
punches and then slams the boy
against my front fender—all in the time
it takes me to come forward and grab
the bully by the belt. Bully is bigger
but I have carpenter arms.
Dangling a hammer from my fingers, I say
If you touch that boy again, EVER,
I will hunt you down and smash your balls
into a million pieces, you pile of feces.
The son's hand is broken halfway backwards
so I drive him pell-mell to Stanford Emergency
and call Gilda who is in LA for the day.
Thank you for being there, she says.
You can bill me for the extra time, she says.
Then I hear her tongue clucking through the phone.
Jesus, Gilda says, *what kind of mother am I?*

The drama queen daughter leaves first,
becomes an actress, you may have heard of her.
I convert her bedroom to a fitness room
that somehow retains the fertile aroma of teen girl.
The posters and photos tacked to the wall
leave so many holes, pricks of idolatry,
I have to re-coat with plaster.
Gilda works out every day, looks great.

The athlete-nerd son leaves last,
now a biologist in Africa,
you may have watched him on National Geographic.
I dismantle the boy's elevated platform bed,
the rails and ladder above a study desk nicely crafted
without nails or screws by blond Scandinavians
using blond Scandinavian lumber.
Disassembled, the structure of a boyhood
fills the back of my pickup as I bring it home,
good wood for someday. For something.

Gilda remarks that her empty nest is too big
for a woman living alone. *But,* she says,
it stores the scenes of my life. The thought of leaving
this house gives me an ache in my breast.
Or, she laughs, *maybe it's cancer.*

A year later, a message on my phone
from her daughter in Hollywood:
Thank you for all you did for my mom.
The memorial service will be held
in her beloved garden.
Could you please make sure
all the toilets are in working order?

Salvage: The Godless Governor

An eccentric atheist falls in love
with a charismatic woman.
He is elected governor of California.
You may google him if you like.
Taking the Oath of Office, he refuses
to say "so help me God." Next election
he loses by a landslide. In the Great Depression
the charismatic woman, his wife, finds God.
To escape her and her holy ways
he builds a tiny cabin in the mountains.

Half a century later I buy the governor's godless acre
and a swarm of termites, cheap. I evict bugs,
expand and transform the cabin to a full house
with space for family, for children, for dogs—
and perhaps, a holy spirit.

But the garage, built for the governor's pagan Cadillac,
cannot be saved. In demolition I make a pile
of weatherworn redwood siding. My neighbor,
old-timer named Tigg, squints at the planks
and says *Holy moly. I remember that tree.*
Though hunched, tottering on a cane,
Tigg guides me to the stump, eight feet in diameter,
where ferns grow in pockets of decay
surrounded by a ring of younger redwoods—
a fairy circle, offspring of the mother tree.
Tigg was a child when she fell.
Tight grain, he says.
Heartwood so dense. Unmistakable.

In the old trees you count centuries by the inch,
one, two thousand rings of slow growth.
That tree was a sapling when Christ was a sprout.
Tigg points—*Milled right here in town.*
The old La Honda sawmill left a signature,
a distinctive kerf like new moons
along the rough face of each plank.
Moon after moon after moon.

Nail holes in these boards, grease stains,
splashes of paint. A pile of unsightly old lumber.
To Tigg—and so to me—a treasure.
Like finding a trove of fossils.

Grinding with belt sander
I spume mounds of sawdust
where my children play as in a sandbox
coating their flesh to reddish brown,
breathing aroma of old matriarch.
Tigg swears he can detect the haunting scent
of Cadillac oil changes. He hears the echo
of Willy Mays cracking home runs on the radio.
He sees the greasy hands of the Guv,
the shadow of a pinup calendar on the wall.

One of those boards I polish to a glow
like the wet fur of some California bear.
Faint kerf marks linger as pentimento
installed as a windowsill above my staircase.
Tigg examines, approves, thumbs up.
Then he shuffles away, last time I see him alive.
A week later we open the door of his cabin
(never locked), find him where he fell,
alone, heart attack.

The window becomes a shortcut for children.
For dogs. From staircase to play yard
German shepherd and children both
can bypass the back door by scrambling over
the ancient, new-born sill and out
the open window with clattering joy.

Bedlam, but brief.
In a mere quarter-century the nest empties.
Remodeling, upgrading, I resize the window,
install a different frame. The old clambered-upon
wet-bear board I set aside, saved. For something.
Already three lives for that wood:
tree for millennia, siding half a century,
windowsill a quarter. What next?

Salvage: Ghosts

Grandchildren, they come so fast.
To prevent tots from tumbling down stairs,
I build a gate. You may pass through it if you visit.
Here, this blond wood for slats.
Seemingly random in the slats are peg-holes,
relics drilled by blond Scandinavians,
once the bed of a bullied boy.
For trim, this scrap of old redwood,
once a windowsill, once a garage,
once a primeval wonder. Oiled to a glow,
from within I see the spirit of a toddling old man.
In the grain are scrapes from the clambering claws
of dogs, from the blue jean rivets of children
tumbling with glee, from the eccentric kerf
of an ancient sawmill.

What you behold, first glance, are blemishes.
Gouges, punctures and pocks.
A rustic gate.

I tell you it is sacred.
A miracle. Divine.

I am Building a Brace

I am building a brace for the front porch
of my brother who is on the other side
of that door listening with headphones
to a recording of Chinese poetry
(in Mandarin, which he understands)
while he is dying, slowly,
brain cell by brilliant brain cell
in that rocking chair whose joints are creaking,
coming undone.

He no longer remembers his phone number
or how to count change at the grocery store.
He is in denial of any problem as he grows younger,
ever younger shedding years like snake skins
while the crack in the porch grows wider, ever wider
so out here in rain I set four-by-fours upright as posts,
I jerk four-by-eights as beams on my shoulder,
        gripped by my hands
        pushed with my legs
        anchored by my feet
as the useless joists of the deck drop termite shit
onto my eyebrows like taunts of children:
nya nya you can't fix this.
But I can brace it for a while.

Long enough, at least
for my brother to forget ten languages.
I will repair that rocking chair.
I will buy diapers, rubber sheets,
install grab bars in the shower.
I won't let his porch collapse.
I simply won't.

Hippie Highway

At the Owl Cafe, Cloverdale

Betsy the waitress seems so young.
Her small mouth forms an O
when she talks, a circular smile
like a knothole with teeth,
narrow eyes because she's had it tough
but a brightness like the unset sun.
Coffee and spicy apple pie Betsy serves
to the highway patrolman while
everybody in that cafe watches
through the big window
a hitchhiking couple with a dog,
the girl in pigtails and denim overalls
looking innocent and fresh and upfront,
the boy in ponytail, a beard like Spanish moss,
the dog acting goofy like a giant puppy.
A camper truck stops, and they pile in back
to the unknown.

The highway patrolman orders more coffee
and says, "They never learn, do they?"
Betsy smiles, touches his hand,
wishing to find out.

Farmhouse, 1969

That summer in Missouri
a barn cat had kittens.
We poured milk in saucers.
Diarrhea. Vet called us city kids,
said you can't give milk to barn cats.

That summer in Missouri
busy owls left pellets of fur, tiny bones
each morning by the outhouse
saying this could happen
to who, to you.

That summer in Missouri
cows poked heads in the open window
where we lay sweaty on sheets.
They bellowed: *Sun! Up!*
Called us city kids, too.

That summer in Missouri
we skinny-dipped in the muddy Meramec,
washed ourselves under the pump
taking turns with the handle
and then saw a fuzzy screen, Neil Armstrong
bouncing on the moon,
almost as far away.

That summer in Missouri
a neighbor invited us to church.
And by God, he advised, *pick those tomatoes!*
Next day as we sat in chapel
a hailstorm clobbered the roof
of our flower-power microbus
safely packed with red fruit.
Dumb luck? Providence? In appreciation
we joined the little congregation
and nobody called us city kids.

The first (only) time I met Hugh Hefner

Chicago, an alley behind Walton Street I was seeking
food from garbage cans (in 1968 I did such things).
Ugly smoke stank up the air while angry voices
chopped through the exhaust fan of a
restaurant kitchen when I passed out.

Cradled in female arms, female scent, I heard
"He's just a kid and he's sorta dead."
Opening my eyes I saw bunny ears and the top half
of bulging brown breasts. A name tag said JUDIT.
I mumbled "I'm almost twenty-one."
Judit said "He ain't dead yet." She dropped me
to the bricks where my head went BAM.

Next come Gucci loafers worn by a man
in a smartly tailored trench coat
standing over me lipping a pipe like a smug asshole
except for teardrops brimming—from the smoke,
I thought. He asked what did I think I was doing.
So I told him I'd hitched for two days
wherever the truckers were going and whatever
they'd feed me which wasn't much.
He seemed to like that answer.
He dabbed his cheeks and eyes with a hanky,
snapped his fingers at a cook
who brought me a sirloin on a big plate
while he kept nibbling on the pipe stem
as I told him I was on Spring Break from a crappy job
driving a school bus, no career plans
except I was a writer, and he said
"You mean you want to be an author?"

I said "No, I mean I can't stop writing even if I want."
He seemed to like that answer, too.
"Send me stories that change this shitty world," he said.
I asked who he was.
He introduced himself just as jiggly Judit
came out and said he was needed inside,
the police wanted to close the place down.
He gave her butt a squeeze and hurried away.
I asked Judit what was happening and she said
Martin Luther King had been assassinated,
the city was on fire and seeing as how I was white
and kind of naive I'd best get the hell out of town.
"You mean he's DEAD?" I said.
"Yeah," she said, "and everybody's pissed."

Judit handed me green money, a few twenties.
"From Hef," she said.
I said "I want to stay and talk to you."
She laughed and said "I'm almost thirty-one."
She wrote a phone number on an order slip.
From a Greyhound bus window on the Skyway
paid with Hef's money I saw flames of the riot,
smoke like a photo of Berlin at war's end.

King and Hef, both had ideals.
King had the better ones.
Hef became a caricature, icky. Fame can do that.
Nobody needed to kill him.

Once, I called Judit's number. A man answered.
"Don't ever call here again," he said.

Omaha, U.S.A.

She says she's from Omaha
so I tell her I passed through once on a hitchhike and—
> *Wait,* she says,
> *what do you mean 'on a hitchhike'?*

She has a friendly heart-shaped smile
so I explain I was just bumming around
on Christmas break from college and—
> *Wait,* she says,
> *you didn't go home for Christmas?*

So I explain I was in search of real America
when a trucker dropped me downtown near the river,
an old brick building with a sign that said ROOMS $3
but the little man at the window demands $4.50
to stay all night, the $3 would be for an hour.
I only have $4.75 to my name but I pay and—
> *Wait,* she says,
> *why didn't you have more money?*

So I explain how it was all part of finding real America
which I thought was fistfights and factories and I was
searching for fossilized ciggie butts of Kerouac and
Cassady still littering roadside ditches—
> *Wait,* she says,
> *who is Kerouac and Cassady?*

Real Americans, I say, which maybe I wished I was.
My hotel room was a putrid mattress,
one thin blanket, broken window, door without a lock,
froze my ass, not much sleep with shouting all night
and somebody peed on my door—
>   *Wait,* she says,
>   *did you see any other part of Omaha?*

Her eyes look sad with big brown pity.
No, I say, I hit the road before sunrise.
>   *Wow,* she says,
>   *if you went to my house,*
>   *my parents might hate you*
>   *but as my friend they'd make you a bed,*
>   *and I promise they'd serve you*
>   *some good grass-fed Nebraska beef.*

Is that the real America? I ask.
>   *Duh,* she says.
>   *Did you find anything better?*

Official Licensed Poet

I go to the hiring hall for poets
but a bouncer at the door demands to see my license.
"What license?" I ask.
Don't play dumb, he says. *No license, no entry.*
"But I'm a poet," I say.
Lemme ask, he says. *You got poems in the New Yorker?*
"No," I say.
You got the MFA?
"No."
You got awards? Prizes?
"Just a bowling trophy," I say. "How do I get a license?"
*You got to take classes, conferences, workshops taught
by Official Poetry Teachers. Then, the license.*
So: no hire, I'm illegit.
Oh well. The pay was shit.

I keep the day job. Go around the city. Open mics.
Reciting poems to small groups.
Out loud. For free.
The audiences, they never ask to see a license.
After the reading a few men, always men,
come up to me and say
I don't really like poetry but I like your stuff.
Always, they call it *stuff.*
Women say they like it, too, but without
the disclaimer and they don't call it *stuff.*
Face it, guys are uncomfortable with poetry.
Me, too.

I find a wise woman. She's got the MFA,
the publications, the awards.
An Official Licensed Poet if ever there be.
She says, *I met that same bouncer.*
Everybody meets the bouncer.
She walks with me to the Hiring Hall.
The bouncer blocks the door.
With a quick move, martial art,
she flips the bouncer to the floor.
She says, *A poet is a verb, not a noun.*
A person writing a poem is a poet.
A person not writing a poem is something else.
You'll find her poems in anthologies of Great Lit.
She says, *By the way, the pay is still shit.*

So listen, bouncer: I write stuff, therefore I am.
My license. Now scram.

Why Idaho

Boise on-ramp. Honda Civic, yellow.
Leaning out the shotgun window a dog's head,
golden pointed ears. The brown wet nose
sniffs toward me, snorts. The driver a woman
in mirror shades orders the dog to the back seat.
Says I can ride as far as Pocatello
since Goldie says I'm okay.
As we roll past potato fields she says

"Goldie killed a man when I lived in New Jersey.
His name was Louis.
I didn't train Goldie to kill.
Got her from a shelter.
The man Louis broke into my room
where I was sleeping. He told me
not to say a word or he'd slash my throat.
Goldie from a crouch leaped over the bed.
Ripped his throat. So fast!
Blood on the blanket. Pools.
You know how blood smells? Sour.
Like bad Italian food. Like fake Parmesan.

"They said I had to put Goldie down.
That's why we live in Idaho.
Don't worry, she's friendly if you are.
Here, give her a biscuit. Place it on your palm.
Don't hold it in your fingers or she might—
Look! She likes you.
She's licking your hand."

Spring Rain was Her Name

To behold her would wash your eyes.
Her child she named Bebop Blue
but we called him Bop.
Spring Rain and child, they lived
in a rusty old van. At school she volunteered
teaching the Great Books to ragamuffins
with a wild passion until the day
she parked the van, middle of the highway,
locked the doors blocking traffic
behind mandala curtains screaming
too much evil—*Evil!*—in life.
At the uncautious sheriff
she slashed a knife.

Bop disappeared wherever kids go
until thirty-two years later I'm talking to a guy,
he's planting roses while I'm installing
outdoor lights. "My name's Bop," he says
with a handshake, "I used to live around here."
Far out! So I ask about Spring Rain.
"Her name's Jane," he says and shows me a photo.
Gray hair, a beaming smile. So fresh. Like new.
No anger has Bop. A man at peace,
at low pay digging holes for roses
to please rich people's noses.
He learned the Great Books.
"She's a good grandmother to my kids," he says,
"though we never leave them alone."
To behold her would wash your eyes.

Sparkling Shana

Shana learns young to raise herself.
To smile for survival.
Mom sings in LA nightclubs,
loves cats and gin and lunatic theories, also men
who stink of tobacco but pay the rent.
They don't treat Shana kindly.

Mom has a plan to save the world
though she can't explain except to Ronald Reagan
so Mom rides a bus from LA to the White House,
a call from the DC jail: *You be good, Shana.*
I'll be back as soon as I can.

Shana rides in Grandad's pickup across deserts
to Texas where she finds kindness and horses
until a pinto tosses her onto her spine.
Then Grandad's new woman hisses *He's mine.*

Shana hitches to Frisco where she's a bent flower
in bright clothing. With Texan good sense by day
she works as a secretary to a garbage company,
insurance benefit. Nights, it's like a costume party.

Weekends, no costume at the beach
with killer weed and wearing a smile when
she meets a man on horseback who clicks. Like love.
He's lacking in kindness but Shana follows for a year
until the drugs go crazy—his for fun, hers for pain.
He gets prison, big time. She gets
probation and a baby girl.

Two years on welfare, an insult but keeping clean
and with the innate wisdom of a survivor
she marries her chiropractor. Not love, not exactly,
not at first. No click. But it's kindness.

Later, love.
Now she manages the office. Her back
has never felt better. In school the little girl blossoms,
grows tall, so smart. See Shana smile.

More often than we might think,
the grinding of the earth creates a diamond.
Lovely. Hard. Sometimes flawed.
And she sparkles.

Sometimes rural America looks like crap

especially in sleet when you're driving
a vintage VW bus with a weak heater
north from Chesapeake Bay.
It's all gray. The railroad tracks.
The town with three bars and no cafe.

With my six-year-old son riding shotgun,
shivering, toweling the windshield,
I'm looking for some dead ancestor's homestead
but we'd settle for a warm drink and a cheeseburger.
At a gas station we get heat-lamped hot dogs,
a basket of backyard apples (tart and crunchy),
their last pair of gloves (I wear left, my son right)
and directions.

Here, this dirt road. Cows plod in front of us
sloshing their udders until a wet dog chases them away.
There, a barn missing half its wood. Rock foundation.

We poke around. A red pickup stops.
A farm boy asks what we're doing. He says
somebody's been stealing the weathered siding.
"Not me," I tell him, and we make to leave.
He tells me the land we're looking for is under water
since they built the Conowingo Dam
and we're in Pennsylvania now, anyway.
There's no sign when you cross the line.

We pass a dead horse, vultures. Farmhouses
surrounded by trash and cars. A hawk glaring
from a bare tree. To get home it'll be two hours
by freeway at the mercy of tractor-trailers
through the tunnel under Baltimore Harbor.
"Sorry," I say to my son.
"This is *great,*" he says.

From me he got the explorer gene.
Icy road, we take it easy.
Somehow, a fine day.

Your Spirit is a Shadow

He was a beatnik.
I was a hippie.
Just a few years made the difference.
In the final years I was caretaker.
Me with flower-power tendencies
paid bills, ordered meals, lit candles
for a cranky beatnik atheist
who used to sing in the opera.
Could be a setup for a TV sitcom,
my brother and me.

He hated religion, loved philosophy.
We would argue about spirit.
I said we all have a spirit that lives on after we die.
He wasn't buying it and kept challenging me:
"What is spirit? What do you mean?"
I told him your spirit is like a shadow
except instead of darkness, we cast light.
As the sunset neared on his life,
I could sense his spirit growing larger.
He denied it to the end and I love him for that.

We burned the body, scattered the ashes.
I sense his presence still
and he is scowling, shaking his head.

Your spirit is a shadow
     lingering
          made of light

Your spirit is a shadow
     growing longer
          into night

Your spirit is a shadow
     none can capture
          all can see

Your spirit is a shadow
          set free

Hippie Highway

This tie-dyed microbus has aged
half a century just like you.
In mist with no working wiper
needing a sub at the wheel
you stop for hitchhikers near Mendocino.
They reject the ride, call it junk.
Punks.

At the Oaks Cafe you're the only customer
along with six kids riding tricycles around the tables
while two moms help themselves to beer
from the cooler. The cook who is also the waitress
has stars in her nose and owns one of the kids.
She calls you "Sir" until you make her stop.
You ask if the pie is fresh and she says, "No,
it's as stale as our coffee. Have a brownie.
They're, um, spiced."

Now it's dark as you drive down 101
with headlamps dim as doobie tips,
not even aimed right, some big rig might not see
before plowing you like dirt so you follow
a camper truck painted in mushrooms
that glow and fade as your lights work and don't.
The funky camper seems to feel a kinship.
He sets a slow rhythm, a two-vehicle conga line
across the Golden Gate.
They are your shield and protector,
the driver with beard and leather hat,
the affectionate woman beside him
glancing back from time to time
between kisses. Chugging slowly home
let it be known there are loving angels,
yet today, on the hippie highway.

Call of Nature

A Month of Storms Like Holy Wrath

Saturation. Land is liquid. Hills flow.
Trees ease onto highways
where they stand, roots and all,
like stubborn jaywalkers.
Houses slide. Roads dip
as mountains shift, shrug,
slough away the works of man.

Our gurgling crawdad stream
rushes with logs, eats the soil,
snatches a cabin, sweeps away
a full-grown man filling his lungs
with mud, breaking his body
to dump him among driftwood.

Wind whipsaws a Douglas fir
until thirty-six inches of solid trunk
snap with a sound like a bomb.
Roof shatters. Walls pop.
Upstairs become downstairs.
A skylight takes flight like a Frisbee
and lands unbroken in mud.
Clothes hang on branches.
Fir needles fill the kitchen sink.
The refrigerator lies on its side,
food sprawled over the splintered floor.

How fragile are the works of man
yet somehow inside the crushed house
a telephone is ringing.
Who, dear Lord, is calling?

Catamount, Late Summer

Come with me. Here's
the secret trail. At the edge
of the potato field, crouch through
the barbed wire fence. Enter
the maple forest, the green oven.
Bake, slowly rise like a gingerbread figure.
Release rivulets of sweat.
This is nothing, the foothill.

Listen: the purr, the burble, the rush,
the small canyon of Catamount
Creek. Remove boots, splash yourself.
Splash me. Cup water in hands
to pour over the face. Let water dribble
inside the shirt, drip to the shorts.
Relish the shock of cold
against hot parts.

Work uphill now, at last
out of the trees into the land of
wild blueberry. Pluck, taste
tiny nut-like explosions of blue,
so intense, so different from store-bought.
Gorge, let fingers and tongue
turn garish. Fill pockets.

Climb with me now among rocky
outcrops like stair steps to the Funnel,
a crevice where from below
you push my bottom, then from above
I pull your hand. Emerge to a view
of valley, farmland, wrinkles of mountains
like folds of flesh. How far we've come.
This is the false top.

Catch your breath, embrace the vista,
then follow me in a scramble up bare granite,
farther than you'd think, no trail marked
on the endless stone but simply
navigate toward the opposite of gravity,
upward, to at last a bald dome
chilled by blasts of breeze.

At the top, sit with me, our backs against
the windbreak of a boulder.
Empty your pockets of blueberries. Nibble,
share—above the hawks,
among the blue chain of peaks
beyond your outstretched tired feet.
Appreciate your muscles
in exhaustion and exhilaration.
We have made love to this mountain.

Hear a sound like a sigh from waves of
alpine grass in the fading warmth
of a lowering sun. Rest.
After this, the return
is so easy.

Bitterroot Storm

You made it. Hell of a drive.
Now in the cabin you're shivery, raw.
Floorboards tremble.
Branches pelt the roof.
Rain blows under the door.
Phone? Lamp? Radio?
All wires, dead.
Power will be out for days.

You fetch wood,
build a fire, heat water,
light lanterns named Aladdin.
Play guitar, help the neighbor start her car.
Clinging to this mountain
your cabin is a spot of warm
in a dark storm.
You are power.

Wolf, Wildlife Refuge

Gandy the tawny wolf picks me
from a crowd of gawkers at the fence,
leans in sniffing, studying. Gus the keeper says
Gandy's keying on your aftershave.
Nope. I'm gray-bearded, unshaven.

I ask if Gandy is an old wolf.
You're very perceptive, Gus says.
Nope. Saw it in his stiff movements. Like mine.

I seem the only one engaging Gus or Gandy
while spectators aim phones, capturing us
in digital cages.

Gus says wolves can smell cancer or arthritis,
helps them select which moose
to cull from the herd.

Gus says Gandy still acts like
the alpha wolf, hates competition.
They keep him penned separately
so no one gets mauled.

Gandy steps to the fence.
From his throat, a low growl.
Like an anvil, the snout.
My joints ache.
And Gandy stares at me. Hard.

The pilot cuts power to the engines

as we're crossing the snowy Sierra
and the plane drifts lower
across the fertile valley of rivers
to the airport by the bay.

My Uber driver has a straggly beard,
calico flesh with spots of white like half-moons,
eyes with a touch of the wild
like you see in malamutes
with their wolf-ancestor DNA
who should be watched around small children.

He asks "Where from?"
I say "Just back from DC."
"Did you see *him?*"
"Yes."
The driver mutters a curse, then smiles.
"Come," he says.
"Where?" I ask.

He drives me south through suburbs like a Lego set
then west among mountains like misty breasts
into a forest dense as bear fur
to a redwood tree with a burn scar so large
he can drive inside it and park.
"Get out" he says.

Beneath my feet are beer cans, cigarette butts.
Scent of charred wood mixes with urine.
It smells like the city I just left.
"Come," he says.

We climb spiral stairs within the trunk
and walk out onto a massive limb
high above the other treetops,
wisps of fog blowing from the blue Pacific
in breeze that ruffles our hair
with the fragrance of salt-spray, of photosynthesis,
of prowling pumas and fresh unfolding fern.
A pair of red-tailed hawks soar spirals in an updraft.

"Here" he says.
"Yes" I say.
"You will pay me now."
And gladly, I do.

My bony butt sits directly over

the San Andreas Fault on a wooden
bench next to a soccer field
where in 1989 a movement under
Mount Loma Prieta—the World Series
Quake—knocked my striker

son to the dirt. From his knees he
watched oceanic waves lifting sod,
lifting his knees in rhythm
to the pulse of a planet shifting tectonic
plates bringing Los Angeles two meters
closer to San Francisco. Today a red-tailed

hawk soars overhead. White egrets
depart the apple orchard flapping for the
willows muffling the creek. Gangly wild turkeys
scavenge among windfall apples
for bugs, worms, while muttering turkey-tunes
like a funky feathered choir.

In the parking lot a gray-faced man rests in
an old Chevy wagon of about the same age,
feet out the window in ragged Adidas,
plastic sheet over the roof, open tailgate, home.
Hey, he says. *Spare change?*
Quietly beats the heart of Earth, at rest.

Call of Nature

Past midnight we're in bed
when to our ears two owls
sing outside the window
huh-hoo, hoo, hoo
among the oaks, by starshine.
A duet, art, they are surely aware.
Harmony is no accident,
a matter of constant adjustment
by minds with intent.

Side by side we lie. I call to you *huh-hoo*
and you respond to me *hoo-hoo.*
From outside:
Huh-huh-huh-huh hoo, hoo, hoo.
You laugh, we embrace, bed creaks. Then silence.
We spooked them.

Face to face, we wait. Scarcely breathe. No sound.
Perhaps, like us, together they press.
Perhaps they nest.
After minutes, softly from outside:
Huh-hoo.
Huh-hoo, hoo, hoo.
One calls, one responds,
then voices blend, girl and boy,
for harmony,
for joy.

The Opposite of Hate

Her Breasts

The white-haired doddering gentle old man
in the crushing silence of the public library
blinking through spectacles
writes with shaking hands
in a pocket notebook
unaware that he is muttering to himself
Her breasts… her breasts…

Eyes peer over books. Pencils pause
except the old man's. Fingers
mark pages. We await,
expectant, puzzled. He has pulled a dusty volume
from the shelf of his memory
and, still writing, whispers, hissing
Her breasts…

I want to know: was it in moonlight?
Hurried? Forbidden?
Dear woman, do you know that after half a century
not only your lover but a whole reading room
of men and women are sharing—are in awe of—
your stunning warmth
Her breasts! Her breasts!

Jean, fifth grade

was a practical girl
with a bony nose
skinny as a straw, gap in her teeth
dusky brown skin.

Chinese, somebody said.
Mexican, somebody else.
Never asked, now I wonder.
I was a practical boy.

She wore dull clothes
but she was bright,
smart as my dog, maybe smarter
always danced in bare feet.

Those days, maybe still, boys lined
one side, girls the other.
I'd head straight to Jean, offer my hand
because we danced good together.

Black hair bunched in a rubber band,
no bow or ribbon except her smile.
Girls teased, Jean scowled but
always took my hand.

Nothing planned, it just happened.
Dancing we hardly talked,
I was shy.
Without music we stayed apart.

Sixth grade she was gone.
You don't know you're in love
first time
until you do.

Upward Through Bubbles

In swimsuits which means
essentially naked
the girls gather at the bridge
gasping giggling
budding bouncing
as they climb over the steel rail
stand at the outside edge
hold hands
scream

and jump
the scary plunge
to cool water, Donner Creek where
toe-touching the sandy bottom
they burst upward through bubbles
to sunlight, to air
whipping hair
with laughter, relief,
stronger now,
sweet courage
with a touch of spice.

Frog-kicking to shore
they smile
at the baggy-legged boys
who dared them
standing hands in pockets
smaller now
feigning indifference
unworthy of their loveliness.

Just sayin'

You sure you want a prince?
Actually, dragons are hardworking,
faithful and honest, long term.
Maybe not so good-looking but
it takes skill to breathe all that fire.
He keeps the house warm.
The kids can bounce on his tail.
Prince Charming is an idiot. Look at
all the great women he ignores
while out chasing dragons.

Soft-core Cold War

Pulpy paperbacks. Lurid covers. Cheap.
My father bought them. Read them
with a serious frown. Every evening
he'd bring home more. Threw nothing away.
Filled shelf after shelf, then box after cardboard box
so I had plenty to read, from Henry Miller
to Mickey Spillane to hack-job smut
nurturing my puberty.

Nikita Khrushchev was thumping his shoe.
My childhood dreams were of nukes
aimed straight at my bedroom.
The old man built a bomb shelter in the basement
where Mom banished the cartons of books.
Summers when air dripped of heat,
in the company of an old infested cat
I explored the cool underground.
On book boxes I sat by shelves of dry food,
a gas mask. In candlelight I sucked up words,
hopping like another flea along the glorious
hairy underbelly of American literature.

I started high school; they shot JFK.
A new topic for dreams: I noticed this girl
dark as the Potomac, bright as starshine.
Smart, freckled, wholesome as Cheerios
yet a mystery no detective had solved.
I took her to the bomb shelter. She took me
to her eyes, her lips, her touch thermonuclear,
her words softer than the softest porn,
her library, volumes yet to be born.

Life Lesson

The boy rides the backpack,
big silent eyes absorbing this fresh morning
when we hear brakes squeal. *Yelp!*
A doggy yelp. Me jogging, boy bouncing,
we find a white dog hit by a car,
blood spurting. Car gone.

We follow the dog to a front porch.
I know this house, the bedroom with curtains open
where once on a night walk I with then-newborn son
stopped among others, sidewalk passersby,
watching as a woman danced bare to a mirror.
"Somebody should tell her," a man said.
"She knows," a woman said.

White dog is whining, raining blood.
I knock. Door opens. A kid. "My mom's in bed."
TV cartoons. Loud ones. Mayhem.
"Would you wake her?"

She comes out in a see-through nightgown
looking sleepy and annoyed, says her dog
never goes to the road. "Every day," I say.
She twitches my son's nose in the backpack
and says, "Hi there, cutie," then winks at me
while her dog is bleeding all over the carpet.

My job is done. I turn to leave.
Her kid is crying about the blood.
She shouts, "Turn that crap off!"
In the backpack my son watches, wide quiet eyes,
whatever one learns at the age of six months
of dogs and blood and sexy women.
Some day I hope he'll explain.

To My Daughter Who Was Never Born

I know you are a daughter because
we already had a boy, a girl, a boy.
It was a girl's turn when two cells
in a womb chanced not to meet.

Now here's a prom date waiting, corsage in hand,
at our door. Aren't you ready yet? Our family,
never big on proms. Or dressing up.
Will you dance in blue jeans?

As parents, we made it hard.
You, only seven when your mom got cancer.
Not easy. I'm sorry for that.

In your fourteenth year, daughter,
we blew up. Yes, I came down hard on you.
Stealing a car is serious trouble.
But I promise not to dwell on that. Except to say
I secretly admire your gumption to steal
the candy of a billionaire's spoiled brat,
to without lessons drive that Jag to San Diego
to free a dolphin who, it turned out, didn't want
to leave his private tank where fish appeared
like magic twice a day precisely timed.
Some souls prefer order. Not you, not me, this family,
beyond the bedrock expectations: Get an education.
Be kind. Don't steal cars to rescue dolphins.

Here, daughter, some fish.
Next year again I will lose you who I never had
as you burst from your tank swimming,
leaping the prow of this aging boat
with such grace, such hope,
your home the ageless sea.

Ski Cabin

Naked, sipping wine
under stars so silent,
our breath crackles coming in,
then floats out in frosty clouds.

Fully tenderized, we step dripping
from hot tub to deck
where fingertips on doorknob
discover frigid metal, unturning.
A self-locking door!
Towels and clothes left inside for warmth.
Hopping barefoot in snow we test each window.
Our bodies are steaming.

Already we shiver.
"Maybe the neighbors have a key," I say.
We are on a cul-de-sac of four cabins, all dark.
Would somebody rise out of bed and open
the door to a man clothed only in goosebumps?
They could call the police while we freeze to death
because where is the nearest cop
in the Sierra Nevada at midnight?
And what is the jail sentence
for public inadvertent nudity?

I fear frost-bite in delicate regions.
"I'll have to break a window," I say.
Triple-glaze, I see.
"Please be careful," she says shivering, gasping.
"I'll stand back and throw a rock," I say,
and do, with strength I didn't know I had
heaving a hunk of stone the size of a football
which makes an astonishing sound
like a gunshot of glass.

"Watch your step," she says.
In the pitch-black I can't tell shards from
pine cones but at first footfall something
pricks, draws blood, as a floodlight erupts
from the cabin next door. A young man
stands in the doorway wearing only a sweatshirt
(Nevada Wolf Pack) while holding a baseball bat,
and then a young woman's voice says
"Put away the bat, Deion, and *help* them."
The woman steps out wearing flip-flops,
a bathrobe, and says, "You don't look like
the bad guys. Come in and get warm."

And that is how we meet our new friends
Deion and Kimani who are just normal folks
because, really,
wouldn't you do the same?

The Opposite of Hate

Singing in the shower.

Playmate.
Roller skate. Rhyme
is the opposite of hate.

Balloons.
The only thing you should ever blow up
is a balloon.

And skinny-dipping.
Creekside, hot afternoon.
Buck-naked is the opposite of hate.

On Call

I am in bed, midnight, when the doctor calls.
She says my brother is in the emergency room
with high blood sugar, dehydration, another stroke.
        She wants guidelines.

Dementia.
He cannot feed himself or even smile.
Yet he lights up whenever I arrive—
        you can sense it in his eyes.

As a child I chased after him on a tricycle.
He taught me baseball, rebellion, girls.
Taught me to drive our old Studebaker.
Sent me letters from California until at last
I followed, too. Now he leads
        on this new path.

"No heroic measures," I say. "Do not resuscitate."
"Okay," the doctor says, "what about a feeding tube?"

When a heart stops, it is as if the body decided to die.
But if the body cannot swallow? Or think?
He slowly starves. Who decided that?

To the black bedroom a soft light comes,
headlights passing. Rain is dripping.
Dogs are sleeping on the floor, one with a gentle snore.
My wife, head propped on hand, lies on her side,
watching. In this quiet night with the doctor's breath
in my ear I am an incompetent god,
        but the only one on call.

Birthnight

I was born on August 19, 1947.
I have proof: a hospital bill
handwritten in script, blue ink,
from Sibley Hospital in Washington, DC
for one childbirth, $48 stamped PAID.
My mom probably picked up the tab.
Dad was careless with pennies and sperm.

On that swampy-hot summer evening
Dad must have driven us home in the
wood-sided Willys, no seat belts,
bouncing beside the Potomac River
so broad and so quiet,
the B&O railroad tracks, the coal trains
like black snakes, the C&O canal
in moonlight, the sycamores
heavy with leaves.

In the crumbling brick house
of too few rooms I would sleep
in a closet, for fourteen years my bedroom
was a closet and yet I would grow,
I would leave pennies on the tracks,
swim the river, walk every step of the canal
all the way to West Virginia with a girl
who would hold my hand and kiss my lips
and lie with me among sycamores,
with her I would grow to be a man, a father,
grandfather of wonders
who kayak many a river,
who climb many a sycamore,
setting many a penny
on many a track.

While You Were Gone

While you were gone we had an anti-war summer
on a farm in Missouri, missed Woodstock
but had our own mud. Finished college.

While you were gone we drove across Nebraska
in that little green bug to the gray Pacific
where I floundered through jobs. Dad remarried,
then died—diabetes, stroke. She got the house.

While you were gone we moved to a hippie enclave
with a big metal mailbox next to a cow pasture
among friends who chose not to wear clothes.

While you were gone we had a boy. First thing
we put the baby in the mailbox, took a photo
of his head sticking out, sent the postcard
stamped "Special Delivery" to everybody alive.

While you were gone I cut my hair,
started construction work, right livelihood,
stopped floundering. Thank fatherhood.

While you were gone we had a baby girl
who grew to your spittin' image
and one more baby boy who now
has a beard like Dad's—you'd laugh.

While you were gone
I got older than you.
See you soon.

Some Day, Grandson

Infant of painful belly
sleeps only when held, gently bounced,
seeking skin contact, the family scent,
flesh to flesh. My daughter so tired,
new mother, must rest.

Men need to do things. At least, I do.
The porch rail remains half-built,
the truck idles roughly, not today's chore.
Just as I once rocked my daughter, now
her babe sleeps with warm little cheek
against my stubbly old,
hot puffs of breath
on my grainy neck.

Some day, grandson, you may wear
my scent of sweat, sawdust, motor oil.
For now you smell of milk, mommy, peace.
Life is so basic with a baby—
doing nothing, giving comfort,
the work of love.

The Waiting Room

Surgeons must be morning people.
We arrive under fading stars.
Behind this strip mall a rooster crows.

In the lobby she fills out a form, signs, signs again.
A hug, and she's gone.
The door shuts with a clack, loud latch.

Stanford tried; treatment failed.
My grandmother would say "If the good doctor
can't cure you, find the less good doctor."

Outside, sky lightens purple, orange, pink
over a Taco Bell next to a rollerskating rink
where vultures perch on lamp posts.

It's called a Procedure Center.
Free coffee while you wait, real half and half.
A fan rumbles, blowing heat.

A little man, bald, half my age,
runs down the hall wearing scrubs.
A cute nurse pops in, tells me the procedure
will take 15 minutes, then they'll watch for recovery.
She'll probably be fine.
Just wait.

my lady of scars

in her lovely form
they poke holes
through shoulder
spine, neck, breasts
removing this
correcting that

from her body has come
endless nurture
some pleasure
three babies
four cancers
the cuts, sewn tight
the children, grown tall

she cooks
without recipe
she has faith
without dogma
she has dogs
of wild faith

That Summer

She's about your age you guess,
leaning over a triple sink,
sleeves rolled up in a baggy sweatshirt,
elbow-deep in soapy water
washing ninety-three soup bowls
(she counts, you learn) in the camp kitchen
when you deliver a load of maple firewood
in Pop's wheezer Chevy truck.
She's one of the camp kids, city kids,
they make them wash dishes as punishment
but what could she do wrong?
Her hair is a swirl on top
like black soft-serve ice cream
with one lock loose over the forehead.
Cheeks shiny.
She reaches in rubber gloves for a can
of Comet Cleanser on a shelf over the sink
(stretching, exposing belly, unaware)
when she sees you and tries to push
the straggle of hair from her face
leaving little bubbles among the freckles.
She smiles.
Her teeth are straighter than yours.
Sparkle eyes, green, and she says,
"You want a potato chip?"
How it begins.

About the Author

Joe Cottonwood has built or repaired hundreds of houses in his day job as carpenter/contractor in the Santa Cruz Mountains of California. He is the author of the underground novel *Famous Potatoes* and many books for children as well as the award-winning memoir *99 Jobs: Blood Sweat and Houses*. His previous books of poetry are *Son of a Poet* and *Foggy Dog: Poems of the Pacific Coast*.

www.ingramcontent.com/pod-product-compliance
Lightning Source LLC
Chambersburg PA
CBHW022013080426
42733CB00007B/590